T0160717

tomaž

τomaž

A YOUNG LIFE OF
TOMAŽ ŠALAMUN

CONSTRUCTED BY
JOSHUA BECKMAN
FROM CONVERSATIONS
AND INTERVIEWS

WAVE BOOKS
SEATTLE AND
NEW YORK

Published by Wave Books

www.wavepoetry.com

Copyright © 2021 by Joshua Beckman

and the Estate of Tomaž Šalamun

All rights reserved

Wave Books titles are distributed to the trade by

Consortium Book Sales and Distribution

Phone: 800-283-3572 / SAN 631-760X

Library of Congress Cataloging-in-Publication Data

Names: Beckman, Joshua, 1971– author, compiler, translator.

Šalamun, Tomaž, author.

Title: Tomaž / Tomaž Šalamun, Joshua Beckman.

Description: First edition. | Seattle : Wave Books, [2021]

Identifiers: LCCN 2021012558 | ISBN 9781950268481 (paperback)

Subjects: LCGFT: Poetry.

Classification: LCC PS3552.E2839 T66 2021 | DDC 811/.54—dc23

LC record available at https://lccn.loc.gov/2021012558

Designed by Crisis

Printed in the United States of America

9 8 7 6 5 4 3 2 1

First Edition

tomaž

Have you ever seen God,

how he comes running at 2:30 exactly

responsibility responsibility

you don't draw me near the beginning or the end

immovable and tied

instead of dangling your legs just like that

responsibility responsibility

the world without nature

the world without conversation

irresponsible are the trees as they grow

and what has a word to do with it

the sun doesn't need it to set

nor the sky which is blue and nothing else

who did God ask

when he created the butterfly as it is

when he could have made its legs five inches in diameter

responsibility responsibility

baroque sustenance of the people.

I'm usually
somehow shy
about reading
my young
poems

because they don't
go with this
body anymore

it was in '64
so probably I was twenty-three
or maybe twenty-two

I don't remember
no I started one in '63

so I was twenty-four
or twenty-three

no

no art

I was just a student
of Art History

maybe I should start from my youth
from my childhood if you want

we came to
well my father was
in a way
politically punished

we had to leave Ljubljana

because he was very critical
of some vaccine

(a Russian vaccine
that was given to children)

he talked about this bad drug
and because he was a leftist

but never a Communist
and had people who liked him
they said, we should put you in jail
but the best we can do is
just hide you somewhere

so we went
to Herzegovina
to Mostar

and when the political situation
changed and Tito went against Stalin
then my father could come back to Slovenia

but not to Ljubljana
not to the central place

so we came to Koper
which was Capodistria

and we arrived in '49
and this was still practically
an Italian town

I remember we lived in the old part

there were two families
who were Slovenians
and all the others
the entire street Italians

and this was a small town
of a thousand people
and my mother taught me piano
when I was five
and the school opened
after two years

so when the school opened
I had some kind of advantage
and I was pushed as somebody
who had really
who had really great

and you know I did feel
because I had this

this is something big
this is art

and some friends of the family came
when I was ten eleven and they said

you cannot keep this kid here

you should go to Warsaw
or to Leningrad

this provincial
his provincial teacher
you are wasting his time

so I played
but the pressure built on me
and I had this incredible stage fright

and it happened once
when I had to play
in front of an audience
I just stopped
blank

and
I had to
go down from
the stage

it was an incredible shame

this huge
psychological torture
because they had
really treated me
like a wunderkind
and gave me lessons

harmony and contrapuntals

as someone who would study
in a musical academy

and one of my teachers
was a really hard alcoholic
a very well-known composer
but very unhappy
with this small Koper position

and so when I was twelve
I was also a rower
and we were competing
and we were training for regattas

and my father said to me

no, you cannot train twice a day
because this will really be damaging for your heart
I don't allow this

so I never touched
the piano in my life again
as the response
to both of these pressures

I was twelve
and this was the reaction
to my father's
law

and this
was the end

I really never touched
the piano again

a little bit I played guitar
very dilettantish
but that was it

there were four of us
I was the first one

my sister was more intellectual
but we were popular

actually very popular
because of my father

because the Italians loved him

he was a pediatrician

I remember there was a carnival
we walked in the small town

Masks

they just danced around
my father and chanted

Viva dottore!! Viva dottore!!

you know I felt
I really felt protected
I was a quite sheltered happy kid

TOMAŽ PO-
SLUŠA —ALI
ČITA?

In the last year of high school
I hoped then this girl
who everybody in the class was in love with
I hoped that if I would arrange a trip
so our class could go to Greece
if I would collect money for the whole class
then I may have some chances
somehow with her

So what did I do?

I said we will make a literary journal
but this was just a pretense

I told the others don't waste paper
if you have to write a poem
make it short
because I need all this paper
for ads

I collected ads
from shoemakers
and politicians

you know I just went door to door
and collected enough money
to go to Greece

this was 1960
and it just didn't happen in Yugoslavia
in communist times
that a whole class
would go to Greece

this is something very special
and I behaved as someone
who prohibited practically *all* literature
in favor of ads
because I needed money

and yes we went
and we were on the boat
and on the Dalmatian coast
a man came
and she fell in love
with this person

when I returned from the trip
my Chemistry professor

(twice-removed cousin of my mother)
fell in love with me
and she was five six years older

you know
I was very
my sexual upbringing
was very very slow
so basically when we danced
and she said at the end
she was sad

I didn't understand then
so many years to realize

so then I went to Ljubljana to study
and left my sailing boat behind

I stopped sailing because
in the last two years of high school
we sailed around

we were eight once
in this Mediterranean basin
we went to regattas

63 SMO IMELI ŽE BARKO
   Z MOTORJEM

and this was my life
but I was the second man on the boat
not the captain
I didn't know what to do
I didn't want to think about my life

What should I do?
What should I study?

I was sailing
I was rowing
I was a boy scout

you know the thought that I will somehow
have to study Medicine
I didn't want to think about it

and then I enrolled
in Medicine
and realized after a week
I'm cheating myself
and stopped

and still
completely insecure

I enrolled in Art History
because my mother was an art historian

and to punish myself for the gesture
I enrolled also in History
because the History professor
was our family friend
and he was known
as the most ferocious
demanding professor

because
I wanted to come closer to art
I enrolled in Architecture
for one year and then

in my exams
something happened

I was questioned

I was questioned
and just without any word

I remember incredibly the texture
as I would stare now

for life
I would remember
all this perfect tissue

I couldn't utter a word

such a defeat
such a zero point
in my existential situation

trying this
trying that

first cheating and trying
and then

Dane Zajc

came into our seminar
and read poetry

Dane was about
ten years older than me
he was incredibly handsome

he had some kind of really dark presence
some kind of really traumatic presence

his poems
were also very audacious and dark
which was not the art in communist times

he had some kind of special mythology around him
we all knew that he was a great poet

and followed him
and admired him

not thinking
not wanting
to become a poet
or even trying to write poetry

I was in the third year
and Dane had read his poems
and I was I was absolutely

I remember when I saw him
cross the street my knees went weak

because it was such
a charismatic experience

and my best friend
Braco Rotar
started to write poetry
maybe three weeks before

he started to write poetry
and for me this was like Braco
my close friend
became something
in between human and god

we lived together
and these two influences
Dane and Braco
produced or cooked something
in me

so that my first poems
really dropped
like stones
from the sky

and everything else
five six poems in a row
and I knew that this
this is something really strange

I thought maybe I'm sick
and actually these were the first
lines that stayed

One day you are aware the hand exists
already for ages it has known it exists
swollen with its handness
it stares at you vaguely used to being a hand
but what now what will the consequences be
who will define the new borders
you didn't understand well said the hand
you're not you I'm the hand spreading
then I'm an arm
I'm pale and I sing I sing loud
and make my bed
stop for once with your tiny yellowish thought
you're not pale you didn't sing you didn't sing loud
nor make your bed
because YOU ARE NOT YOU, I AM THE HAND
the world is the decay of the world
but what now what will the consequences be

so these lines fell
and my reaction was

that I was afraid

that maybe
this was some kind of
mental disorder

but also I felt that
this is something important

as I had
one time
as a child

what happened to me
as I was playing piano
and had the big hopes
to become a great artist

hhhhhhhhhhh

that is something
it really touched me

this is what I've done from inside
which came from some kind of deep
inside which was blocked really
from my twelfth to twenty-second year

then I was sure

Braco
had written
more poems than me

like ten more than me

I thought
he's a genius

so I took him
so I went with him
he was very shy
to Perspektive
the main cultural journal

we walked there
I walked with him there
and said this is a genius
you should publish him

so they looked at his poems
and gave an answer

and their answer was
yes!

and they asked me
Why did you come?
Are you writing poems too?
and I said yes

so they said
bring bring us
what you
have written

so we were both published
in the same issue

and at that time
there were several other magazines
but this was really the most important

and they published
maybe every year one name

one new name in poetry
or maybe eventually two

and this journal was also
constantly on the border of
being too transgressive
or not too transgressive
for the political powers

but they need some kind of lab
mind lab for themselves
so I was paid for the first six poems
I was paid more than the monthly salary
of my mother who was
a librarian
and high up

I remember dinner

I got thirty thousand dinars
and my mother's salary was twenty-seven
and my father
who was director of all of the hospitals
in the area
got seventy thousand

so I practically got half the salary
of the director of hospitals
with six hundred beds

but you know
this money
this in a way was
trying to pacify
and to cultivate
those dangerous minds

My siblings
because I was the oldest
my sister
one year younger
was still in Koper
and my mother arranged
through her friend
that I come to Ljubljana
and I had great rooms
for cheap

and then I met my girlfriend
who I first remember
when I was a boy scout

she was a girl scout
from Trieste

Trieste was Italy
but they were living Slovenian

so I fell in love
and then she was my girlfriend
for five years
for four years

she studied Architecture
she was my age
and it was under her influence
I enrolled in Architecture

Tatjana

she was also a pianist
she finished conservatory

I was very proud that she was a pianist
I liked to listen to her and we visited many times

we were constantly at concerts
and it was very strange

I was proud that Tatjana was a pianist
but you know I was just part of the culture
nothing more
because I would not

my piano
was definitely
closed forever

I was with her
until the end of my studies
and then at the end of my studies
I went with my best friend
and one of his friends
in a small car
to Greece

while Tatjana was busy
finishing her degree

and we spent almost a month
or maybe five weeks in Greece

my friend was French from Belgium
because when I was young

my father was in Paris
on a kind of post together
with other doctors
and they decided to exchange kids

so I went to Brussels when I was sixteen
which was totally shocking to me

you can imagine this was '57
from poor communist world
to come to Brussels
to a rich Jewish intellectual tradition
and family with a private clinic
and the sister of the doctor's wife
was running Shell for Europe

so we traveled around France together
and when I came back
I was so mad at my parents
that they conceived me in such a hole
in such poverty

and really the most depressing
was that they were cultivated
and kind of asked me

Who are your important men?

and I said

Plečnik Kocbek Prešeren

total silence

for sure you have somebody

Croatians have
Hungarians have
Bulgarians have

so I felt
I don't want to be
an orphan in Europe

I had no idea
but just was worried
that I live in such a small space
unknown
squeezed politically
nationally
and I really thought this could

this has to be changed
one day

so we went to Greece
then after Greece
I went to the army for twelve months
in Bosnia

I was in the army
and fourteen days before the army ended
I got a letter from Tatjana
explaining that she will marry my friend
and she realized
you know that her ambitions are bigger
than to live in such a small hole in Slovenia
with a local poet hero
and she hoped
that I would understand

so in the Yugoslav National Army
they were very good
they were very humanist
and they gave me a special man
a soldier who walked close to me because
I was almost really suicidal

this was such an incredible shock for me
that I was in pain of course
that kind of betrayal

I always hoped
a new poem would happen
but I also always thought
that this is maybe
the last poem which happened to me

and it was everything
it was very dramatic you know
because I couldn't start
I could only hope
and when it came
it came as a
strong earthquake

and my early poems
had many many
these poems are really linked
with my youth
around the sea in Koper

you know I use Italian words
because when we were rowers

when we sail
all the names we use
around the boat
the small screws were Italian
because this was the tradition

Slovenians
also had names
but they were not used that much
and they didn't sound that authentic
because you know the Slovenian coast
is really small

but I do remember
(this is very important)
when we came to one regatta
because if you see the land
it's Monfalcone
and about twenty kilometers
it's Trieste the town
and then you go south
you come to Muggia

Trieste
was first part of

the Austro-Hungarian Empire
never Venice
even Muggia
so the eastern coast
was basically Italian
but where Slovenians really came
to the sea
and where sailors and fishermen
and so on

in this part
which is now Italy
and the place where I grew up
Koper

Koper
Isola Piran
Capodistria
Isola Pirano

they were basically Italian towns
that became Yugoslavian
after the Second World War

and what happened
to my mother

when fascism
started in Trieste
in 1920

even 2 years
before Mussolini
had the great speech in Rome

those protofascists
in Trieste
were the most horrible
because they were so nationalist
that it was obvious
they burned down
the Slovenian Cultural Home

and this is a sign
so whoever could leave
did leave

and my grandparents left
with my mother
for Yugoslavia

because Fascists behaved horribly
because after the war

Italy switched
a big part of Slovenia and Croatia
became Italy

so one third of Slovenia
happened to be in Italy
and in Italy
Slovenian
was a prohibited
language

and Fascists changed the name

if they would stay
my mother born Gulič
would have to be
Gouli or Goulini

and really spit in the mouth
of kids
if they heard them talk
in the Slovenian language

the only place to speak it
was in the church

the priests still had masses
in Slovenian

the half brother
of my nana was a priest

he went through first
went through Fascists who squeezed him
and also then after the Second World War
because of the communist state
the Communists were not
at all kind to priests

I put this picture
of my mother
on the back of my first book
Poker

it says

this is a picture of my mother

and I made a book
for my mother

to je moja mama

when I was six
which I still have

my sister had written a book
for her birthday

she was five
and I had this small book
and we put them together
for her present

and strangely enough
that book
the structure of that book
is like Poker
not the poems
but like the thing

I'll find nails,
long nails,
and hammer them into my body.
Very gently,
very slowly,

and this poem
this poem

is already the battle
being a middle-class bourgeoisie
in the future

and so I am protecting my
sacred poetry place even against
my beloved women

I'll find nails,
long nails,
and hammer them into my body.
Very gently,
very slowly,
it will take more time.
I will draw a precise plan.
I will cover myself every day,
two square inches of cloth for example.

Then I will burn everything.
It will burn for a long time.
It will burn for days.
Only the nails will remain,
all soldered, all rusty.
And so I will stay.
And so I will survive.

this is definitely the influence of
a sculpture which was wood
with many many nails in that wood
then somehow burned

and it's you know
these are all very
it's very close to existentialism
you know
it is close to Antonioni
it's close to Sartre

it's from Antonioni
I don't know
probably
I've seen it before

I only recall
Monica Vitti
reminded me of Tatjana

this incredible truth
the truth how we live
what is danger
what is the danger of civilization

I didn't like
Zabriskie Point
for example

because I thought
now he got too old
he is paranoid

he has the same prejudices
against America
as I had
from my parents
before I came to America

my parents were leftists
they never became Communists
because my father

he sheltered his colleagues
in high school
who were already Communists
through the influence of his father
who was an influential lawyer
in a small town

Ptuj

he had some kind of
relation to the court

so this is the reason
why communism really crushed my father
when he went against the Russians
but still they had some respect
not to jail him

you know
my mother
was also a kind of Marxist
half Marxist
a great idealist
she finished Art History
but then she started to be a nurse
then they
my father
still as a student doctor
they went together
and helped women
in the less developed areas

this generation
was very responsive

I was proud of them
but they were so strict

for example my mother
when we camped
she insisted that the grass be
left very carefully
and when we left the camp
no piece of paper
would be thrown away
nobody nobody would smoke
nobody would have a glass of wine or something

and I thought
this is too much
my friends who sail
the Mediterranean
they were kind of
it's closer to
charm
or to whatever
to how people look

it's more
it's upper-class bourgeois corruption

rich people have yachts
and they went to
they didn't finish university
they studied two years
and then became
directors
of the local bank

they were all rich
became quite rich

Christine
was the daughter
of our Polish friends
who I also was kind of
she was partly in love with me
I was you know
it was when I was with Tatjana

Moi, je m'en fous des poètes, Christine.
Now I eat salad.

If someone comes,
he should not come in as I'm sleeping.
You know it too, Christine

who came from afar.
I keep telling you,
close the door
this stench of food
will spread all over the apartment.

I feel Mediterranean
which means in a way almost more Italian
than the rural Slovenians
who wouldn't understand the sea
and when I see here for example
when I quote those peasants
who come to the sea
every night
aqua dolce

the old fishermen said
true
like locusts on Sunday they come rushing
and dip their legs in it
legs in it
legs in it

this is poking fun
at rural Slovenian peasants
the sea and the beauty of the Mediterranean

this is already the influence of Eliot
because Eliot was for the first time
translated in 1960 by Veno Taufer
and it had an incredible impact
on me

It was immensely hot
this I must tell you

We walk in a herd like cattle
some devout
some not so
as one's whimsy goes

It was immensely hot
this I must tell you

Sonny drives around in a carriage for two hundred lira
c'est quand même drôle tout ça
and St. Francis appears with his birds
steps out of the can and closes the lid
poverello con suoi occhi ingenui
amazing how much I like
this last constructive chap
in the history of Europe

I learned Italian in Perugia

as students of Art History
we went to Italy
from museum to museum

we went to see Giotto's frescoes at Assisi
and this was written
from the memory of that trip
when I was back in Slovenia
pretty soon after that
quite immediately after that
when I call St. Francis the last you know
and this already I had got from Pound

change line to include some French
or to jump from one language to another
and I was very proud of my French
which was the only language that I spoke
the only foreign language that I spoke without an accent

when I was younger
people didn't know if I was French
even they might have thought that I'm Swiss
this was how I was international

and Ginsberg too
had an incredible impact

I remember that moment
when I read Howl
in Croatian translation
in the Zagreb railway station

So it goes
best of all are the little mushrooms
little mushrooms in the soup
nothing nothing nothing nothing

pheeooooo one little mushroom

one green parsley in tuxedo
then darkness for a long long time
then they run to find a cleaner
responsible for everything
nothing nothing nothing nothing

pheeooooo one little mushroom more

for the younger poets
this was some kind of

very memorable thing
it's kind of transgressive

all this should have happened
in the twenties

but because Slovenia was
so provincial
the poetics didn't explode
the only one was Kosovel

Kosovel was at the level
but his poems were not released
his avant-garde poems his
Integrali
was not released until
'67
because of the pressure
of my Poker

this is '66
Integrali came out in '67
and before they were not known
partly there were a few poems
translated into French

and I read French Kosovel

which I really liked
but I didn't follow it
but in a way maybe

there are three or four poems
which I have read in French
before I published Poker

but no
those cannot be the influence
you know
maybe

It's strange how you sink, kangaroo
and if I show you a straw
you mostly only stare at me

you never thought
why cows do not sprout
but are always born
as calves, kangaroo

cool when you learned to swim
that's a fact

but some shadows were there
from the day of your birth
you didn't eat gorgonzola
there was hair on your fingertips
and something cockadoodledo
was in how you turned around,
were you at all aware,
Caravaggio was a psychopath
cried each time he saw a radish
But where's the way to Mt. Krim, kangaroo

you stole our shoes
you turned around a snipe
you wanted to make slices from time
but time is always time
only, it's in the shadow
it sticks together at the right hour, kangaroo

let's try to say Victor Hugo
Victor Hugo
you see you see it works
could we also say Esplanade

so it is as I thought kangaroo
you may not have typhus exactly
but it's not much better

It's strange how you sink kangaroo
even if I threw you a tractor

I bet you would peel and eat it
but a tractor is not for that kangaroo

and this was seen as a kind of attack
this had some kind of political power
subversive power

as one of my first poems
my Duma '64
enraged some government official
who saw himself in it
and smashed the magazine
and sent me to jail

this was my
five days in jail
it was very big

and when I came out
now I must really be a poet
and this jail made me
in a way
very popular

and people saw me
I was 23

and I do remember a professor
that the most important professor of Comparative Literature
who was basically the main intellectual
he really liked these poems
and in public gathered in reading with students
and talked about this
new level of poetic responsibility
which was really strange
to me

and it all started
because of this letter

this person who was in the central committee
a French Surrealist
had written practically
a love letter to me
on the front page of
Communist

saying look now
something really up-to-date happened
in Slovenian poetry

which made complete confusion for Slovenians
who treated me as a decadent
bourgeois corrupted
by French cousin
and dark power capitalist

and earlier once
I had met this Oskar Davičo
in Rovinj
where he had a house
and we quarreled about Eliot

and he thought this
this is kind of
conservative Catholic
so this is also the reason
he had read my book when it came out

but everything had feedback then
everything every poem

even if Slovenia didn't respond
circles would respond
because there were bigger circles

Belgrade as a center of culture
was much stronger
more open
than Ljubljana
in the
'60s '70s

all the tradition
they had their surrealists before the war
they were winners in the Second World War
one of the main poets became an ambassador in Paris

all this connection
with Simone de Beauvoir
the French leftist

this Yugoslav embassy in Paris
was kind of the ground
for leftist French intellectuals

and the argument about Eliot

Oskar Davičo said that Khlebnikov
or Mandelstam or Mayakovsky
are much stronger poets than Eliot

and at that time I didn't know Williams

this was all new to me
because I studied Art History
because I came to poetry
from basketball and sailing

I knew
French poetry mostly
or Oton Župančič
who was Whitmanian
but I didn't know
because Whitman was so powerful
in all Slavic poets
even though we didn't have Whitman translated
but because Oton Župančič
served in the West as a teacher
with some rich families
he experienced the West
in the beginning of the century
and some came through Kosovel also

Kosovel's mother
you can see how the Slovenian bourgeoisie was
in who had access to something

in a way
even years later when I became
a cultural attaché in New York
and because I was treated by my boss as if
now a drunken poet will be here

and I showed them the
who's who in the world

and I had more lines than
Milan Kučan
the president of Slovenia

Janez Drnovšek
the prime minister

and more lines than the head
of the Academy of Arts and Letters

so Slovenia touched the world
through very little windows

you know and Kosovel's mother
when she was a really little girl

she served in one patrician family in Trieste
which was an international town
the main Austrian port
and where actually my mythology comes from

my grandmother and my mother
started school in Trieste
because Trieste was a big Slovenian town

Slovenians were one third of Trieste
but Trieste had 300,000 people
when Ljubljana had 30,000

and all the land around was Slovenia
so this was basically
this was lungs
and an opened window to the world

Ljubljana was not very open
even now now slowly yes
Ljubljana was somehow
quite homophobic
quite homogenous
and not a very generous town

you know I was attacked in the papers
practically every week

they started to pick one of my lines
and poke fun at it
and describe what they meant
and poke fun at everything

and if my brother
my brother is six years younger
and when he became a student
and somebody called
Šalamun

and my brother
who was definitely
the most handsome Šalamun
stood up

the response was oh
it was not *the* Šalamun

or Metka said
when she was a student
at the academy

and I visited
and people said
ahhh Šalamun Šalamun

so it was maddening
because it was pre-Beatles era
pre–Bob Dylan communist time
poetry has an incredible impact
especially poetry under political duress

and I was happy
but also aware that I shouldn't get corrupt

for example because I constantly
had problems with money in the '60s
a friend thought
that if I would make some kind of gesture
and express some kind of kindness
toward the president of the Academy of Arts
in a statement maybe these personal attacks
on my poetry would slow down

because the president of the Academy of Arts and Sciences
was a pre-war liberal and my grandfather was liberal
and my grandfather was the head of the hunter's society

basically they played cards together
or my grandfather brought him some pheasants

it's an incestuous place

VACATION TIME

I watch my grandfather basking in the sun
under the oleander
or sitting awesome stiff
the way he praises the beekeeper
and says the meal, when will it come
and eats his brunch

glues an envelope
on which is written
Commission for the Investigation
of War Crimes
or simply sleeps
points out the window and says
cut down this tree
this tree brings mosquitos
and Mrs. Abramič comes
and we travel by train
and there is Brežice
and grandfather is nervous

and Rogaška Slatina
and chestnut trees
and a brass band
and Mrs. Senčar plays piano
and we beat time

and we're four
and it won't be easy to change trains
and Jelka cries
because she has lost the green pebble
the most important one
to her little garden gateway
and Cilka steals flowers
and someone was playing with the needle
and the needle bent
the weather will be ruined
but grandpa as if nothing
keeps reading
Flora und Fauna in den Alpen
Flora und Fauna in den Alpen
Flora und Fauna in den Alpen

We talked
and it was it was
the sense that

there are big
you know
Yugoslavia
is not part of the Warsaw Pact
it is much freer
the borders were open
we had passports

it was of course
it was for example after jail
those five days

then I went
with my student colleagues
to Rome

and most of them thought
that I was a secret agent
because I was jailed

but then because of the pressure
they thought that maybe
they smashed me

so in a way it was very tense
it was very very different compared

to Czechoslovakia
or Hungary or Romania
but if you traveled
to Poland
to the Austrian-Czech border
you cannot imagine how it looked

the train stopped
some soldiers were crawling below the train
then customs open every

(knocks on wall)

super excessive
absolute control

and when you crossed the border
they were like puppets
they seemed like post-Holocaust puppets
because everything was so depressed

I was writing in my room
that was the only
I had a huge room
and I was writing in there

Poker

well part of Poker
was written in Kraków
the place where I most wrote was Ljubljana

I don't know if I have ever written anything in Koper

of course I have written Duma
when I was walking near Koper

and I think I have written a few poems in Koper

but the second part of Poker
I have written in Kraków

I lived in a room
that was also organized by a family friend
this was a beautiful bourgeois place
sunny

most of the time
I went to the café
I went to some readings
but mostly to the theater

to the movies
and I met some friends
and mostly I met really beautiful women
that I would go with until the door
and then I'd escape

you know
I was
I was faithful
and then I do remember that the man
he wanted to have a talk with me
and he says that he realizes
that I'm in love
he sees

the Poles speak
they don't say you are
you are not

what would be the word
you are somebody
who really makes chaos

what is the word

it means that you
can't keep your things in order
and he said in a Polish phrase

The gentleman is not caring enough about his order

because I was doing this
making a mess
because it was a great moment
because all my time
I spent in the library
reading Barthes
reading Derrida
reading books
napping
there was time
to see what was going on

I could read poetry
and I could read novels
and I could judge what really interests me
and what interests me less
which I lost now
that time
at that time
I could

this was '67

before Paris

I knew that I would then
have to make a PhD in Art History

You will marry and have kids

and this was the kind of thing
which I as a poet didn't

as a poet I want to be really free

and I wanted to be a poet
and when I was offered
a grant to stay at the university
I said no
and the professor
was very angry

because I just wanted to be a poet
but could not say
I am a poet

a better solution will be to pretend
I will do a PhD and my PhD will be
in French Historical Painting
from the first part of the 19th century
and we will arrange a grant
for Paris and for Rome

so I went to Paris

I was very
I was devastated
because I had lost Tatjana
and I felt tremendously old
but then a friend of mine she invited me
to their sun house
and she was
I basically
my sexual upbringing
is horrible you know
like you are absolutely responsible with women
if you kiss the woman you are responsible
you have to marry her
you cannot compromise women

so she seduced me
and she was my girlfriend
for a year and a half

let me explain
for example the situation
in Paris in '67
she was really rich
and I had my student grant
she also had a student grant
and I insisted I will eat with the students
because I want to live the life that I have earned

I was her hundred and thirty-seventh man
she was probably mostly
it was a total sexual occasion
my three months in Paris
I practically spent in bed

I went to Rome
and she could have but I said no
you have a grant for Paris
we were three months in Paris
I went to Rome
we were the same age

twenty-seven

in Rome
I received a postcard
I fell in love and I am marrying

she fell in love
with a nineteen-year-old
Athenian gigolo

but I arrived in Rome
with a letter of introduction
from the museum director
to meet artists

a huge office

white silk

enormous dog

and when I walked toward her table
this dog was really mythical
Felliniesque

I gave her the letter

she opened it
and said oh young soul
you come from my friend

what do you want

oh yes I will connect you

and she called up a very famous sculptor

and said oh I have one very elegant young soul

take care of him

take him in

show him the art

in two days I was drinking with

Pino Pascali

who was one of my living gods
he was a really powerful sculptor
who very soon was dead from a motorcycle accident

I spent the time with this group of artists

great parties with patrician families

these Roman villas half blocks
with all this aristocracy
and I joined

and I invited Milenko Matanović

who was one of the avant-garde
one of the members
of the group
OHO

I said Milenko come here
to Rome

this is the place for you
because he was the most charming

even when
he came he came
before we exhibited
at MOMA
he went by himself
to New York

and he met Lucy Lippard
and La Monte Young

and he met Patti Smith

he was such a very very charming animal

twenty-three years old

Milenko come here
and I remember I was invited to a party
by a contessa and I said I have invited this friend

and she was shocked
you invited somebody without asking me

oh no no
I said
you will be very satisfied

Alberto Moravia
just came from China
and Alberto came later
and Milenko was already there
and an immediate success
because he was very handsome
and when Alberto Moravia arrived
he was a limping and old man
and he tried to be the center of attention
but Milenko was the center of attention
and Moravia left very soon

so it was

it was great

What was I writing in Rome?

it was supposed to be
a novel from found pieces
copied pieces from journals calendars
this kind of thing

Tomaž Brejc came to Rome
and I asked him to bring

I asked him to bring calendars

if he finds trashy books
for housewives

if he finds what I really have in mind
a boy scout manual

or pieces from old papers
junk

and I was typing this and I didn't finish
what was compressed was thirty pages

playful avant-garde

some memories
from the army
some fragments

this was all stopped

by the black dancer

this hugely marvelous man
because he was in the same pension

I was typing
and he was typing
and we met on the steps
and he said what are you doing
and I said I'm writing a novel

and he said come visit
and I visited him

and he was from
the New York City Ballet
with some kind of sculptures
of the pricks of his friends

he got me high
and we fucked
and this
this was my way
into the gay world

and I was so guilty
and so traumatized

that I escaped from Rome

he gave me some paintings
and I destroyed them

throwing everything away
and escaping

guilt fear
to Ljubljana
and that is when I wrote

Why I Am a Fascist

but that was at the end

I was there for a while
meeting a lot of avant-garde painters

I had a typewriter
this place for example
in Trastevere 68

there were four levels

eight or ten people
he was on the fourth floor
and I was on the first

though we had never really met
I had never even seen him

because either I was in the room writing or in town
and he was in the room writing or in town

but then just when I met him
on the stairs
he invited me to his room

he gave me grass
and pushed me on the bed

he asked me how old do you think I am

and I said twenty-four

an enormous laugh
and he said thirty-seven

so I escaped
I took the train back
from Rome to Ljubljana

I was totally defeated
this man

and I lost two girlfriends
Tatjana and Nina
so I was totally defeated

and when I went to Nina's house

their servant brought me my bag and gave me
my clothes

I will never go again with any rich woman

I traveled the summer around Croatia
and felt incredibly old
and like my life
is really wasted
and I'm a total loser

and then I met Maruška
in October of that year

when young students came to study Art History

and then I danced with Maruška

Maruška

her dress was made by her mother
and Maruška is very
honest modest conditionless

I fell in love
but Maruška had a boyfriend
whom I knew

because he was a young student studying History
and he came to visit me and he was totally devastated
because he knew we slept together

so I hope you marry her

and I said of course

but before all this
in Paris
in the hotel
there was another colleague of mine
who was an art historian
also one lady who married a really rich Italian
and one very very beautiful Italian painter
and me my girlfriend and those two ladies
we walked on Montparnasse

and from the other side came the director
of the Moderna galerija of Ljubljana
and he was with Zoran Mušič
who was the best Slovenian painter ever
and lived in Paris married in Venice
exhibited in the Grand Palace
where Chagall exhibited
when he was alive

and Zoran Mušič
we became friends
he was an incredible father figure

he was tall
he was elegant
he lived in Paris

he was a great painter
and I adored him

and the director of the gallery
said why don't you come work for me
and I will give you something called Atelier 69
and you could do whatever you want

so great

I had a job

and when I came back from Rome

I was assistant curator at the Moderna galerija

with my own inside institution

What did I do

?

OHO

I exhibited

Marko Pogačnik

Andraž Šalamun

Milenko Matanović

David Nez

400

people came

so this was a very big deal

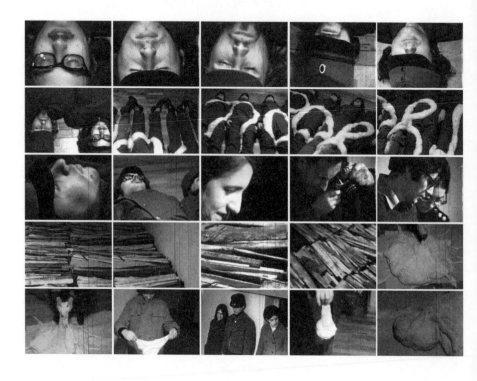

MILENKO MATANOVIĆ / TOMAŽ ŠALAMUN

TŠ   milenko matanović is the biggest impostor living
      he is a bitch, a wretch, a nincompoop
      he is a chump
      he picks his nose
      he's such a dreadful chump that one can only yawn
      milenko matanović has ears and mange
      he's a fascist he wears makeup
      he's a chump impostor with curls in his hair
      he's the general secretary of the fascist party
      he's a chump
      he's the biggest living idiot
      he lies and equivocates so much that everything he says amounts
          to one
      outrageous lie
      he flies through the air and nonetheless squints
      he eats flies that he picks and scrapes
      he is scum
      he grew up crooked and he'll die crooked
      he's a despicable impotent wet fish and even slow to stink
      milenko matanović will wind up in a grave
      he is scum
      i know everything about you and there's nothing i can ask you

MM   ask me what i'm working on

TŠ   what are you working on

MM   i'm pondering my life's work

TŠ   i'm pondering my life's work too

MM   what will your life's work be

TŠ   bread

MM   i'm going to divert the sava river to the adriatic sea

TŠ   i'll haul the sand

MM   inside me lies the entire european tradition, what do you exhibit

TŠ   inside me lies the entire european tradition, i exhibit brick and
     hay

MM   i exhibit ten roman hillocks. what is the conceptual level

TŠ   i'd like all the contingencies that go with it

MM   no, i wouldn't, what are you going to do

TŠ   i'll build out a gallery, i'll buy a bus, a bus driver, i'll drive passengers
     around the exhibition space. i'll plow the soil in front of the gal-
     lery and sow wheat

MM   i'll exhibit outside, my work has a social dimension

TŠ   what should i ask you

MM   ask me what the social dimension is

TŠ   what is the social dimension

Andraž

is my brother

and I remember earlier meeting

Iztok Geister
Marko Pogačnik
and those two guys
already had some kind of a secret

they started in high school
and Marko
who was basically
a conceptual artist

exhibited himself in
a small town in
1959

they tried to punish him
but this was a big political scandal
and the director of the high school
lost his position

these two guys
a gesture of freedom
very very powerful
in the communist world

I knew about the case
I liked them

they were
a little bit younger
and when I arranged the exhibit
for the other OHO guys
of course I couldn't exhibit my stuff
because I was a curator

but I exhibited my piece in Kranj
and this piece was banned overnight
they said it was too atrocious a gesture
it was wood on the floor
just wood on the floor

Before
when I published
Poker
I went into the army
and I came out of the army
I didn't write poems in the army

but those libraries in the army
you wouldn't believe

Ovid
Proust

these were great libraries

you know my status in the army
had no connection to my first time in the army

I was already translated in Croatian
and I remember in one Zagreb magazine
there was somebody who attacked me

and my officer in Dobor
in Bosnia
said oh no
you are a young poet
of course they attack you
but you know
it was nothing political
it was nothing
he was just seeing me
as a young poet
so it was okay

and I read a lot

but it was very dangerous
because we were kind of

used as material
which could be exposed
to more severe conditions

I remember that we went
outside of Sarajevo
and it was 41 degrees below zero
and we have to be there
with rifles in the snow

officers would come
very very nervous

because the conditions
were absolutely harsh
and they would be punished
if soldiers would return
with completely frozen fingers
and somebody would
have to be operated on

so this was really on the edge

then the second part
of my time in the army

was in the criminal department
in Sarajevo just criminals

and I thought oh yes now
now it will happen

but I was not sent to the criminals
for political reasons

but because they needed also
twenty percent of the people
who were not drastic criminals
and have them in between
and then I realized
they thought I should be a spy
for the officers

and I said no

so I was thrown much lower
and these were really criminals
so I shoveled coal every day
(this part of my spine)
until one of the criminals
they had their own informal organization

the big boss
and the second in charge
and someone had something
and the big boss came to me
and said
I see you are an honest person
you now inherit the position
of the one who is not corrupt

and you will help people
how not to get under martial law
or you will write letters
to the unfaithful wife
or
my wife
my wife will come
you must write to her for me

and they respected me
and I was covered by this organization
they said this was really
Šalamun's Law

and three times a day

chooock chooock chooock

they yelled the names

here here here
everybody

I was covered by these criminals
I could go to town in the evening
and when they said
Šalamun
someone else would say
over here

and the officer would calm down
because there were two kinds of power

and at the end of my second time
I could go to dinner in Sarajevo
I could go to a family friend
take my uniform off
and shower in normal circumstances

I advised the others

I calmed
I tried to coach the person
who was really mad
and really disturbed
not to make the situation
for himself worse

advise him how to behave
these conditions in the jail
how to not be broken
how to be modest
and not provoke power

and I remember
at the end of the army
you are supposed to get civilian clothes
all soldiers take off their uniforms
and get their own clothes back
and the soldier dresses in his own clothes
for the last few weeks

and we wake in the morning and yell

ONLY FIFTEEN DAYS

and then I got my clothes
just a sweater and jeans

and gasp

my god
such a disappointment

my soldier colleagues thought
a person who had the status I had
would not walk in such clothes

the only decent thing was
a cravat and so on

and I remember
how big a disappointment I was

after the army
I didn't write for about six seven months
then I went to the house in the country
where my mother's family comes from
and in those socialist times

there was toilet paper
but people also just
cut up and used
newspapers

so I'm in this wooden toilet
this outhouse
and looking at
a little cut up piece of newspaper

and I read it and

awwwwwwwwww

this is poetry

so I copied it

most of my second book
half of this book is found

what caught my eye
for example

Which is your beloved color?
My beloved color is yellow

Would you wear a wig if your hair fell out overnight?
If my hair fell out, yes I would wear a wig

We heard you were visiting Portugal,
could you tell us about your impressions?
Portugal is a small country
People are dressed well

Was it hot?
Yes
It was hot in the sun
Also in the shade it was hot

some were taken
from the Slovenian newspaper in Trieste
this is the list of who married in
the last week or last month

representative Massimo Bianchi and official Luciano Carrera

baristo Roberto Lella and housewife Graziela Vrech

driver Enrico Marsetti and salesperson Floridia Ruggeriero

the book didn't have a name
but people called it

The Purpose of the Cloak

The purpose of the cloak is the cave pits

The purpose of the cloak is a pen

this is completely taken
oh well nothing is complete
this is
this for example
these lines are just copied from one novel
or this is mine

I started
in the outhouse and then went looking
for some other pieces that attacked me

Mums are colored with glycerin

The bread exists

plus above described with a vector
plus below described with a vector

wine exists

What do you like the best in your life?
Peace I love the best in my life

Would you go as a missionary?
I think I would go as a missionary

But I would have to think

What disturbed you the most the last time?
I'm not really sure
I couldn't say what at the moment

Do you feel the consequence of the Second World War?

I do remember that a soldier jumped on

and this is a real memory
my first dated memory
September '43
when Italy collapsed
and an Italian soldier
was in Ljubljana
Ljubljana was under the Italians

this happy Italian soldier
jumped on

and destroyed
the gate latch
and he smashed the gate
with happiness
that the war was over
and this
was my first memory

I have to notice that the best pictures from the churches in Piran
are still treasured in Italy

and we really want to have them back
in the place where they belong

which is a huge irony
because Piran was really an Italian town
before the war
when Piran became Yugoslavia

I see this book
Are you the author?

Do people ascribe to you the sentence:

The day is bright and the night is dark?

so I had written
The Purpose of the Cloak

I had stopped
but it was like one day
I would fall back

and then I started to write

I was writing writing writing writing writing

this was before March 1970

my daughter
Ana
was born
in March
1970

I was writing
while waiting for her

when I still was in my conceptual phase

in Ljubljana

in Maruška's parents' house
in the suburbs

she was thirty
and was a student

I was thirty-three

but I had to leave
the OHO group

their leader was in the army
when I came to them
as a socializer
and also as an artist
when I put this
new group together

I would decide
when we will exhibit

which gallery in Yugoslavia

and then the leader
came back from the army

and they had meetings
at three o'clock in the morning
in some alley in Slovenia

so I couldn't do it

I was the only one
who was about to start a family

they were all younger

then I left

I was lucky
that Penguin published
in 1970
New Writing in Yugoslavia
with a few of my poems

which helped me
to get into the International Writing Program
in Iowa

so I flew to Iowa but
before I flew to Iowa

a Slovenian lecturer of English in Ljubljana
said if you go to America
you should look for
Anselm Hollo

he had his first book in Finland
then hippie flower voice in British poetry
working for BBC

and when the BBC wanted to promote him
to some higher administrative position

he said fuck you
and went to America

so he has to be somewhere in America
you should look for him

try to find him
you will like him

so I came alone to America
Maruška and Ana
came about eight days later

I came to
Cedar Rapids
and from Cedar Rapids
I was driven to

the Mayflower

which is the building
where all the international writers
were put

and I signed the lease
and then walked toward
Iowa City

a little bit
a mile and a half away

and I went to one bar
and it seemed strange

and I went to another bar
which was also quite empty

but there was
a group of people
and they laughed

and among them an older guy

and they laughed
then they asked me

and I said
I'm in the International Writing Program
and they said they were poets

they were drunk

so the older one
who was their teacher
proposed to drive me back
to the Mayflower

but he hit something
and the police came
and asked for his papers
and he said

Anselm Hollo

oh!

he was the head of the translation department

and so when I would go in the morning
or when I was writing
in the cafeteria
Anselm helped me

spending time with Anselm
mostly writing like crazy
mostly enjoying
America

Bob Perelman
was there and drove me
to his house in
Dayton, Ohio
and we went to
Martha's Vineyard

and one day in Iowa
the tragedy was that Bob had a car

a $300 car
and I was driving

going on the highway
we had an accident

and in the car was
Bob Perelman
Barrett Watten
and myself

and I was driving the car

and Barrett Watten's leg was hurt
and his leg was in plaster

and I was the guilty one
because I tried to pass one truck
in the snow

and the first
you know we were on the highway
somebody came

and
I had this guilt
I was guilty from that

Bob Perelman

Bob's energy was so open

Bob was the best dancer
he was nineteen years old

I was reading American poetry

I discovered

Three Poems

John Ashbery

which turned my head around

and I remembered
when I was an exhibitor
at the Museum of Modern Art
with OHO

in '69

Kynaston McShine said
someone wanted to interview me

and I said
please no interviews

and he gave the name
and now when I discovered
Three Poems

I called Kynaston McShine

when you said that somebody
should interview me

he said yes it was
John Ashbery

so this is the reason why
on the way back

we stopped in New York

with Maruška
and Bob Perelman
and Francie

I called John Ashbery

and he said yes
come have lunch

and he was very open
and said do you have a roof
where do you sleep

and he said
come tomorrow

two lunches
these lunches
were such a mythical point
for me

and years later
at the 92nd St. Y

Jim Tate said to John
I guess you would remember
Tomaž Šalamun

you had those two great lunches together
in '73

and John
with his angelic eyes
walked to me and said
I don't recall

devastated
devastated

it must have been twenty years
just a few days in '73

GODS

Gods are Maruška, Ana, Francie,
Bob, people, Josephine, Anselm
and a bunch of kids. Ana and Nora
are driven to kindergarten in Scattergood.

Maruška is reading something on her
belly on the couch. Francie

bathes and soaps herself. Usually
she gets up an hour later.

Bob, I'm thinking, he'll jump to the
typewriter and write poems. Josephine
sings, she walks around the house.

Anselm is obviously sleeping, his
polar day extends deep into the night.
A bunch of children giggle in various schools.

also from Iowa
we went to California

to visit Clark Coolidge

Francie's daughter
was living in Palo Alto

so we found a place in Palo Alto
and I gave a reading

and
Czesław Miłosz
came to the reading

but then they say
why are you bringing this old
fuddy-duddy Slavic person
if you want to be with us

I just didn't want to be only one thing

but it was a great
great time

I adored Bob

it was so lucky
so lucky to be with them

Clark Coolidge

for me at that time
I thought this is the peak
of geopolitical power

world power
in the language

everything
looks like
total crystal

and then there was this
grandson of an American president
which is not completely true
he is like the grand grand nephew
he was like a pope to those guys
he was about ten years older

also
in California
I met

Andrei Codrescu

who at that time
was the young prince
of the Bay Area

I first met him
in Rome in 1969
at a party

he was
a student of Mathematics
and he said you know
I met an American girl
and I'm in love
and I forgot
about Mathematics completely

after that
we returned to Slovenia
but came back the next year

the writing program was only for one year
but I must I must come back

so they enrolled me for a PhD
in Comparative Literature
just for the money
as a way to get back

and I got an F
in the class of a
Greek professor

he gave me his car
his red Mustang
to drive

I was his student
and I was supposed to write something
about Frank O'Hara

he was married
he had kids

but he was partly
after me

you know he gave me his car
and I got an F

and I said oh
I won't make a PhD

but they said
the consequences will come
next year
and by then you will be gone

so with careful footsteps
and some kind of checks
we survived the year
1972 ʼ73

I came back
to Ljubljana in ʼ73
full of myself

also my book in Germany came out
so I stopped first in London
and then in Frankfurt

but my passport was stolen
in the Frankfurt airport

so I flew into Zagreb
and they threw me in jail

thirty-six hours in jail

I was

I really opened myself in
America

and then flat

You lie! You lie!

and they drove me
with the police car half a day
and threw me in the center of Zagreb

we were twelve people
in some kind of

everything was wood
and smelled like urine

and Maruška's father
when the information came to him
of where I was
they released me

but this experience
was quite traumatic because
I realized what communism really was

and I worked very hard as a translator
living at Maruška's parents' house
spending time with Maruška and Ana

not able to translate poetry
but whatever they gave me

Moravia from Italian
Simone de Beauvoir from French

and a lot of shit

The Life of Ho Chi Minh
some stories of Walter de la Mare

but mostly shit

America

my book America
came out in '73
and it was well received

still some conservatives were there

my archenemy
was the president of
the Academy of Art and Science

his attack was
that this was a destruction
it was toilet poetry
this is chaotic

he didn't understand
the complete twentieth century

I was a household name
because of this jail in '64

I was very well accepted
in Belgrade and in Zagreb

so I was absolutely
narcissistic

whatever this was

I tried to decapitate my narcissism
with a poem

but I was unbearable

I survive '74

but Maruška already wanted to separate

they offered me
they tried to

Maruška's father

they would place me
as the translator
of some kind of
Slovenian organization

and I would write some letters

without asking me
they would just place me there
to have a salary

and I said no

I revolted and
then they also

someone wanted to put me on TV
and I said no I don't want to be

and then when David was born
I landed in Ljubljana

I had just enough
to buy flowers
and to go to the hospital

I had to see my son David

I landed on hard ground
and it was really
bad

now there was Ana and David

and I had broken with Maruška
and she was done with me

Fuck you! Don't you get it
you were already gone. And with that
you crumbled like some loathsome
plastic toy. How
terribly boring, this eternal
theme of yours! This vain little system
of painting and usurping living

people! Any woman would go crazy.
You drank my air like the greediest little
toad. Find yourself some Veronica or
Magdalena, if now, too late,
you realize that your conspiracies with
the apostles are unnatural. Nature, you see!
Of course I believed you, and who wouldn't,
before they saw. But slowly you will
realize, or maybe already, that what you were
playing at was kitsch for history, not just for
a woman. Yes, it's better for me now that I am
leaning against other shoulders.
I'm fine. And the thing about "exhaustion,"
I feel sorry for you! Enough with that ridiculous pale
face of yours, with that "suffering," for which
you are not the least bit talented. These black holes
that you draw for yourself are hardly
love or responsibility towards children, but the same
sort of painted background as "your
Maruška" that never was. And print
this, as you have everything else:
You are out of the game.

and when I tried to get a job
any kind of job

they said
go and rest with your father

which means leave here
and go to Koper

so I went to Koper

and I asked to teach French

and I got it
but I had only one course
because I was not supposed to have anything

years before
when I made my BA in Art History
there was an old man a guerrilla
who was asking me something
and he was taking notes

and then here he was now

he was in charge of a school in Istria
and it was this school
which took me

and immediately
the secret police came
and said Šalamun is unemployable

and he said
you were in diapers
when I was a great revolutionary

so I had this half of a teaching job
in an Istrian village

and in the afternoons
I went to a castle
and we worked on frescoes

I stayed in Koper one year

because in the summer
I went to a small island

where Andraž's wife had a house

and there was a young
Sonja Kravanja
and we

and she had

strangely

the old apartment
I had had as a student

and so I came back
to that apartment with her

my old room
and lived there and tried to make it

and I tried

first I went
going door to door
selling encyclopedias

and no one would let me in
except in one house
there were two young people

I showed the encyclopedias
and they said we don't buy this drek

we want Kafka Proust Dane Zajc and Šalamun

and I
couldn't talk

it was so absurd

I went back to my boss and
she was really compassionate

and said Tomaž Šalamun
now I will give you advice

please take it as gold
I will give you golden advice

don't even read our fliers

never go to the homes

go to the factories

at 7:15 with your coffee

go to the factories

at 9:00 when they have a break

go to the room with fifty secretaries
sell them to mothers for their kids

and talk about how books are great treasures

and I made it and I kept doing that
and I was the second best
and they called me
Pharaoh

and I was able to pay debts
and it was a great feeling

I was free

I was not Šalamun

I owned a yellow car

I knew it was a fascist thing

because you stop at the store and you talk and convince
and I felt more and more guilty doing this
and I left

I went to Greece
with Sonja

then also I would continue to travel
and write

when I left America in '73
on the way back I spent fourteen days at Yaddo

now all the books
written in America

Turbines in America

Arena in America

Imre fourth book

back in Yaddo part of Falcon

Druids in Slovenia

Celebration in America

Stars in Slovenia

Angels in Slovenia

On the Tracks of Wild Game
in Slovenia

Asps in Mexico

when I came back to America in '74

I went to Yaddo

I was spaced out
I locked myself in the toilet

I couldn't get out
so I went up through some smaller window
and I realized I was on the roof

please help
I'm on the roof

but at Yaddo
I was able to type

Falcon

just small lines

some poems
which are more substantial

half in Ljubljana
before the major breakdown

On the Tracks of Wild Game
which was devoted to Sonja

Sonja's boyfriend was at the time
in Afghanistan and India

and he was really
fantastically handsome

when he came back
I fell in love with him

this is Sonja's ex-boyfriend
who was my male muse

at the time I had two male muses
first I met Iztok
who totally enchanted me

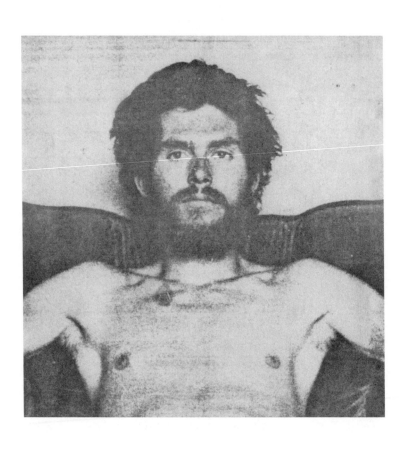

so one was Iztok Osojnik

and one was Sonja's ex-boyfriend

but both of those two
came from Sonja

because Sonja is twelve years younger than me

and all those people were twelve years younger than me

Iztok's role was as someone
who is better than me

so I really adored him

meeting him
and reading him
I do remember when we first

when I really had read
Iztok's manuscript

this is really great
I would like
this is really great

come
we spend
the whole day
together

talking talking talking

and at the end there was
an earthquake in Ljubljana
a real earthquake

and we were absolutely sure
it was because
we met

and because we produced
this kind of energy

and then Iztok went to Japan

he read Whitman

first in Ljubljana
he wanted to publish this manuscript

but they said
it is like Šalamun
we don't need another Šalamun

so we quarreled

a long long correspondence

you know
he published many samizdat books
in Japan

he was constantly traveling

India Hippies Amsterdam Drugs

and this was a time when
I was paying my debts and
I was successful as a salesman

but the thing was
it was difficult
because I couldn't become
a member of a board
of some magazine

my name couldn't be mentioned
on radio or on TV
in Ljubljana

before I went to Mexico I was living
with Sonja in Ljubljana

Ana and David
were in London
and on the way to Mexico in '78

they allowed me
that I would meet them in London
see them

and I do remember
when I stepped into their apartment

it was only
Maruška's new husband
who was kind

and he let me in
and let me see my kids

My one-time wife, Maruška Krese, now lives
at 9 Chatsworth Road, London W5. She has finally found
the right husband and the right house. Exactly as it was
predicted in my text Turbines, p. 56. Children happily
running around a park and sending me pressed
four-leaf clovers.

and then Maruška came
and she had seen how my kids react to me

chhhhhk

total ice total ice

she really hated me

so she prevented constantly
she prevented me from seeing them

so because I was still paranoid politically
and unhappy because of divorce
and I was not able to see my kids

a friend of mine in Belgrade
said don't be so paranoid
you have readers in Slovenia

I know one lady who works
with people who are accepting some grants

I went to see that lady
and that lady said

you have to go to Mexico

Why Mexico?

well she said because
I'm your reader
and I know

and it came to me
I realized
when we were in America
the second time

Bob and Francie
and me and Maruška
wanted to go to Mexico

all these
names of Mexican places

they were already
appearing in my writing

so I'm already there

and she reads this
and says you must go to Mexico
so the poems sent me there

Sonja wanted to marry me
Sonja wanted to have kids

so when I came to Mexico
I said we have to split

In Mexico

I lived a really confused
a half-gay half-confused life

I barely escaped two different women

one family wanted just to place me
as the man because the father died

the male figure
of the one family died
and then they just wanted me

luckily my friend a painter
said you cannot go out
with these girls to have dinner

because the next day
her brother or her cousin
will say now you have to marry her

when I went to Mexico
I just went to freedom
to forget all my troubles

political pressures
communist pressures

I then exploded

and I went
to bars to discos
to gay bars
watched the men

things like that

in the night

in the morning
I just typed

when I arrived I first thought
I should rent a room as a student
in the historical center

so then I asked

and they advised me what to do

I rented a room
in a place that
had about five students
who also had rooms

and I was writing and enjoyed

enjoyed everything

then the moment happens
that Metka's gallerist
who was my old friend

Metka came to her
and she said

I was throwing the I Ching

and the I Ching says
go to see your master
over the ocean

go to see your master
in India

and the gallerist said
go to see Šalamun

and she thought yes
she wanted to travel in Mexico

okay so then she wrote two letters

one to me and one to

her cousin three times removed
who was an American

seeing if he would travel with her
and to me if I would travel with her

and the letter
when I received it
in my student room
it said

Metka Krašovec

I remember
when I was young
we were sitting at a concert
and I remember Metka
and Metka's mother
and Metka reminded me
of my mother somehow

this is just how I remember Metka
Metka and her mother
they were dressed very elegantly

she was a diplomatic child
and when they came to the concert
her mother
was really dressed perfectly
and Metka looked nice

so now
when I saw her name
I knew my life was changed

and the same evening
I went to dinner with somebody
who was a Yugoslav guy

he was a friend of this Slovenian guy

and I fainted
I really fainted

and in the morning
I went to the hotel to talk to Metka

we talked and talked
and then this three-times-removed cousin appeared
a few hours after me

send him away
I said
I will be your guide

and I felt guilty

and we cried
and we drank

after all
you are relatives
you shouldn't marry this cousin

and so we traveled
just the two of us
on buses around Mexico

Metka and I
we made love

now with a woman again

all this gay half-gay things didn't relax me

oh yes

we'll marry

we'll marry on April 11th

when Metka went back
she really cried

we were only
eighteen days together

I got back from the airport

I was really happy

I met
a fortune-teller
who looks at my hands

she says

ahhh
a big thing happens
in your love life

and I say yes

and she says

I am seeing

he is very young
he has dark hair

no
she is a woman!

I still
after two days

no no
first it happened
in the night

I'm going to bed rather early
and someone is knocking on my door
and asks if I have any journals

and I say no
what kind of journals

the next day I see
tall Alejandro below my window

and he comes in the evening
asking if I have any magazines

and we become lovers

and I absolutely lost my mind

and we fucked for days and nights

I was thirty-seven he was twenty-one

Alejandro absolutely messed my head

and I know I will marry on April 11th

so I pushed him down on the bed
and left for Slovenia
to marry Metka

I'm telling her what happened

and for about three days
I didn't function

it was already

we married
we loved each other

and one month
after my marriage
I went back to America

I wrote Ballad for Metka Krašovec

and I went back to visit Alejandro in Mexico

and after I finished
Ballad for Metka Krašovec

I went back to Ljubljana

I went to my dentist
and he said

your palate is all open
I've only ever seen this before
from a man who was driving a car
and killed his wife and two kids
and survived

I was a wreck

and of course Metka was hurt
deeply hurt but still

was able to read this book
as a love book for her

for both

BALLAD FOR METKA KRAŠOVEC
The last time in my life I was left
unconscious was January 4 in the evening
in Mexico. Dr. Sava entertained me
with dinner,
Benito Cereno,
with desert,
with Nolde's youth and the story
of how he became a member of
the Melville Society just before
Borges, while selling
grease for Yugoslavia.
Once we published together in Gradina.
Greetings, Niš!

But I couldn't listen, in fact I was constantly
thinking of the letter that arrived that morning
from Metka Krašovec. Tiny blue letter
written with letters same as here.
I crashed under the table.
Next morning I paid her a visit in the hotel.
First, for her, I crumpled down
Krašovec, this kind of fiancé three times removed.
Immediately he flew back to LA. I don't
like incest. I put a rucksack on my
back. I was constantly thinking why
did I faint. For weeks I was hauling her
on buses and gave her to eat
everything: sacred mushrooms
and Moon Pyramid. With me one sleeps
on hard floors among
scorpions but also there where one plucks
fruit murmuring, you're the color, you're the color.
One day I
cut: with this boy I have
to go to Guatemala, don't you see he appeared to me a
Christ. We were lying on the sand in the
Caribbean, both of us and a Portuguese whose name
I forgot. Go, she said. I sense I will be
crushed but then again
alloyed with you in the light. I

feared. I didn't go anywhere. I took her to sleep
in the motel which was an assembly camp
of white goods for Rio.
Still, she calmly stared, in my eyes.
Better look into heaven, woman,
what are you looking for, I screamed.
Long ago I explained you,
there is nothing left
here. I trembled when we reached
the Pacific. Salina Cruz, ventilating fans,
prisoners weaving a net. Naked I wandered on the sand.
Purple plastic bags, the sky, the body, all
purple. Metka! I said, you cannot
pretend you don't know.
You know! Don't throw yourself in the fire!
Go back to that
Academy. At last they might reproach me,
that I scraped you out. I have to work,
you'll have to travel by yourself, I told
her when we flew back from
Cancún. Why does religion
lose fragrance and taste!
You're crazy! I howled at Carlos, Enrique and
Roberto, do you want me to be kidnapped
by this woman and put back among
Slavs? Why do you look so fresh,

she asked me coming back from
Morelia. And I didn't know anymore
who was a grandma and who was a
wolf. You'll miss committee meetings,
it's time to go back, Metka! And I saw her
to the airport. I feared she would blow it up
with her convulsive crying.
Good-bye! But in fact to me too
the ground started to sink.
My advice to behave as if I were in
Šiška was in fact false.
Long ago. There is nobody in Šiška anymore.
I called her.
I'm coming to marry you.
Come, she said calmly.
Through the receiver I sensed how she was
staring in my eyes.
Very very
tall was the man
who threw for me
tarot cards, an old dame from
Persia turned my palms.
They all said the same thing.
And I was happy. The chill poured
over me. And I

knocked on the door of my

neighbor Alejandro Gallegos Duval

to tell him I'm happy and that

the chill

pours all over me.

Why do we live all so terribly close to each other!

Junoš and Maja said:

he's not as good-looking as you see him, but

strange, he really looks like Metka

Krašovec. I flew to Ljubljana on March 27.

I paid 32 marks for a cab.

Metka was sick and pale.

I gave her back the blood. She didn't allow me

to wear also his ring, she wants me to wear only

hers.

With interest I watched the ushers and my

best man. I finished the precious drinks of

previous guests. Did you, from reading,

at least buy a beautiful tent for

Montenegro? On Snow Mountain two doe

appeared.

I'm here.

My hands beam.

My destiny is America.

I first met Tomaž Šalamun in the late '90s. We were both newly arrived in New York, me variously employed and pretty available, and he the new cultural attaché for the Slovenian state (the most notable part of which was the free use of a photocopier). We met and soon after he invited me to help him translate poems into English. Tomaž first lived in the States in the early '70s and his English was very strong but just shy, he thought, of what he would need to make his poems live in America. At first we would meet after work at a restaurant and eat and go through a handful of poems, but before long I left the city and found myself in Arizona. I was just around the age Tomaž was when he wrote *Poker*, which felt somehow important to us both, and we decided to translate the entire book. I was teaching poetry at the Phoenix YMCA and I would go out and translate on the street corner at the pay phone for hours. We dove in and finished the book before I even made it back to New York. When I did, I moved straight to Staten Island, and for the five years I was there on and off, Tomaž was there on and off. He would get gigs teaching or reading, and would always find his way to Staten Island. He would stay with me for days and I was an early riser but I would wake to find a little line of coffee cups from the downstairs bodega and Tomaž would have a pile of drafts for us to start on already going. By then we had spent time in Slovenia and Italy and would eventually in Brooklyn, Berlin, Alabama, Seattle, and plenty of other places, always working on translations. And for about a decade by mail or over the phone or in person we made translations, hundreds of them, so that our experience of being together was always overflowing with that energy of new things being made, of new things coming into the world. To say Tomaž was a prolific poet is an understatement. In Slovenian there are more than forty volumes, and he spent much of his time working on or encouraging translations. His appetite for it was unquenchable and he often referred to himself as a vampire, but he always met his need for young energy with a young energy of his own. After about ten years our translating slowed down and without being fully aware of it, I had been searching for a project that felt as collaborative and intimate. Eventually I landed on the idea of interviewing him with the goal of creating from the transcripts a long poem about his life, his work, and his muses (because for Tomaž, a muse seemed nearly always to be there in some new person, their presence or absence goading, coaxing, prompting the poems). So we started off on the recordings. Hours would pass and we would slip in and out of the interview, eating and catching up, talking and reading. We floated back into his young life, and as outrageous as his poems can be at times with their living exuberances and dishevelments, he was, in person, more often than not composed like a European gentleman (tucked-in, groomed, and polite). But from the very beginning the unfolding of memories had him in elated revelry, reliving and telling them all. Sadly, *all* was not really where we were going. Two or three years into it, Tomaž began to get sick, and while there was a bit of a reprieve, during which we made our last recording, the book became more focused on his becoming a poet, his opening to art, his intellectual and sexual awakenings. Tomaž died in 2014 and partly out of sadness and partly out of a sense that what was there must not be enough, this book remained mostly an untyped draft for a few years, until that basic pull of missing him had me wanting to dive back in. After turning up a handful of recordings I thought lost (done on a ridiculous variety of devices) and beginning to transcribe, I found lines breaking easily, allowing for fragmented conversational speech as well as the strange drifting parade that is his storytelling style. And running them down the center felt less forceful (less forcefully done on my part) than any other way to have his words on the page. The line through is conversation more than chronology and I think his breath and pace are a bit responsible for the form. I say it this way because the practice of this poem throughout, like translating, was so much about listening, listening and following. It was a kind of getting closer and the sharing of it now feels something like introducing a friend to another.

J. BECKMAN

NOTES AND THANKS

The poems included in this book were all translated by Joshua Beckman and the author. Those from *Poker* were done with help from Ana Jelnikar and published by Ugly Duckling Presse.

The Matanović/Šalamun OHO interview text on pages 91 and 92 was translated by Aleksandar Bošković and Jennifer Zoble and was originally published in translation at the Museum of Modern Art's *post: notes on art in a global context*.

Special thanks to everyone, who each in their different ways helped with this book—Alejandro de Acosta, Heidi Broadhead, Jeff Clark, Primož Čučnik, Blyss Ervin, Peter Gizzi, Metka Krašovec, Milenko Matanović, Miha Maurič, Anthony McCann, Dorotea Fotivec Očić, Iztok Osojnik, Ana Pepelnik, Sabina Povšič, Matthew Rohrer, Ana Šalamun, Katja Lenic Šalamun, Tone Škrjanec, Aleš Šteger, Charlie Wright, Matvei Yankelevich, and Matthew Zapruder.

Many of the images for the book came from Šalamun family albums but also special thanks to Iztok Osojnik, Milenko Matanović, the Moderna galerija/Museum of Modern Art in Ljubljana, and the Marinko Sudac Collection.

page 11 Tomaž with his mother; page 15 Tomaž on boat with his father; page 19 Dane Zajc; page 28 Tomaž; page 35 Tomaž in army; page 41 Tomaž's mother; page 61 Srečko Kosovel; page 81 Milenko Matanović; page 90 Naško Križnar, *Exhibition in Kranj*, 1969; page 93 Milenko Matanović, Andraž Šalamun (facing forward), Marko Pogačnik (the OHO group), Sarajevo, 1970 collection of Moderna galerija, Ljubljana, courtesy of Moderna galerija, Ljubljana; page 96 Tomaž Šalamun installation, *Wood Chips*; page 113 Tomaž, Maruška, and Ana; page 117 Anselm Hollo; page 129 Tomaž, Maruška, and Ana; page 144 Iztok Osojnik; page 149 Tomaž, Ana, and David; page 153 Tomaž and Sonja Kravanja; page 158 Metka Krašovec, 1971 archive of Moderna galerija, Ljubljana, photo courtesy of Moderna galerija, Ljubljana; page 171 Tomaž, Maruška, Ana, and David Nez

The author of more than forty poetry collections, with more than a dozen in English translation, Slovenian poet Tomaž Šalamun (July 4, 1941–December 27, 2014) is considered to be one of the most prominent poets of the Eastern European avant-garde. He published his first collection, Poker, in 1966 at the age of twenty-five. Early in his career, he edited the literary magazine Perspektive, for which he was briefly jailed on political charges. He later studied Art History at the University of Ljubljana before attending the University of Iowa and then becoming a Fulbright Fellow at Columbia University. After he was invited to exhibit his work at the Museum of Modern Art in 1970, Šalamun lived for periods of time in the United States, working as the Slovenian cultural attaché in the 1990s and later teaching at a number of American universities, including the University of Pittsburgh, the University of Massachusetts, and the University of Alabama. Celebrated through many accolades, he was the recipient of the prestigious Jenko Prize and Slovenia's Prešeren and Mladost Prizes. Šalamun passed away on December 27, 2014, in Ljubljana.

Joshua Beckman was born in New Haven, Connecticut. His books include *Animal Days, The Lives of the Poems* and *Three Talks, The Inside of An Apple, Take It, Shake,* and *Your Time Has Come.*